Highly Sensitive

27 Reasons to Love It!

By Ihrén Abrahamsson

©Copyright 2012 Ihrén Abrahamsson

www.ihrenabrahamsson.com

ISBN Paperback 9781479219223

Cover design by Jarle Kavli Jørgensen

http://jarlejorg.foto.no

Model on cover: Cathrine Marie Ellingsen

Dedications

I dedicate this book to my good friends and family. Sensitive or not, you have all put up with my rather headless humor throughout the years.

A good laugh is not only contagious, it also heals!

Table of contents

Preface.. 5

Introduction... 11

1. There is nothing wrong with you............... 14
2. See yourself as the joker, be the wildcard...... 18
3. Enjoy your sensitivity and others will as well... 21
4. Acceptance: your best friend................... 25
5. Laser focus....................................... 29
6. Jump into your emotional boat and rock it... 32
7. Trust your vibes................................. 35
8. Party tricks...................................... 37
9. Not good for you, then dump it............... 39
10. Be the mentor.................................. 43
11. Let yourself flip out and be creative........... 45
12. Sex... 47
13. Use your accuracy............................. 50

14. Love it - it's for free................................ 53

15. Who could possibly be bored?..................... 55

16. Build rapport – because you can............... 58

17. Tell your imaginative stories.................... 60

18. Bring forth your "weirdness".................... 62

19. Talk away about your royal HSP title.......... 64

20. A trillion ways – which one is yours?................67

21. Pioneer the world!.................................69

22. Your right brain's genius – spirituality 72

23. Dance!...76

24. The HSP synonym – intuition................... 78

25. The intelligent influence........................ 80

26. Smile and laugh every day..................... 82

27. Enjoy your recovery............................. 84

28. Summary... 86

Preface

If you have made it to this book I imagine you are either an HSP - highly sensitive person or you know someone who is. Either way, you have come to the right place. You see, all my life I heard that I was too sensitive, too weak, too this and that, and it sure took me a while to grasp all the good stuff about being a Highly Sensitive. And all these years I could never accept the idea that I had been born with this sensitivity for no good reason. So, many years ago I started a ruthless search to find out why. I have since uncovered a lot of information through research and through my own willingness to look at my experiences without judgment, but with the eye of an objective observer. I offer my insights to you with the hope that you will come to a greater understanding and appreciation of what it means to be a Highly Sensitive Person or HSP. I will use the terms interchangeably through-out the rest of the book - for they are both the same.

Did you know that research shows that about 20 % of the global population is blessed by being highly sensitive in one way or the other? I was shocked at first. Then I asked myself why there are so many of us, yet no one seems to talk about it. And what would happen if we started? I know many HSPs have told me that just like my-self, they have felt both embarrassed and shy about their sensitivity and have had difficulties living as HSPs. Those are good reasons to keep quiet. But most people will not even try to understand something unless we start to speak up about who we truly are and that we have different needs.

During my search I was met with a lot of people who put high sensitivity in the same category as: fear, nervousness, bad nerves, weakness, introversion, and depression. They assumed that an HSP was someone who thought too much, too deeply, and too strangely. Being an HSP was equated with being, weird or odd. Certainly not considered "normal." So after a while I simply gave up listening to others because I realized they didn´t have a clue what I was talking about. Instead, I dove deeper into my own traits as an HSP, determined to discover all the juicy parts.

Today, many years later, I am convinced that what we need to do is to accept ourselves as Highly Sensitive´s no matter what others have to say about it. We simply have to step up and allow ourselves to feel and BE completely normal!

I decided to write this book, with some tips that can help you with your own sensitivity or help you understand and support a loved one and accept their needs as an HSP. It´s about time to bring forth the beauty of being an HSP and I want to share all the good things you can do to feel even better.

The understanding of high sensitivity was once hard to grasp, but over the last few years, it has turned into a whisper that is silently swirling over the globe. With this book I hope to explain a few things about the greatness of being an HSP, and, since we are all equal human beings and the traits are universal, I dare to say that it´s possible to apply these tips all over the world.

In the Bible we are encouraged to use the cards we were dealt. Now, as an HSP, I instantly start wondering whether they were really playing cards at the time or if they used it as a metaphor when the Bible was written. This is one of our HSP traits – we question things and like to dig deeper into whatever the subject might be, but I will get back to that later.

No matter where or with whom you play cards, there is some truth in the saying that we have to play out our hand. Though it is not about getting the best cards. It is about using the cards you already have the very best way you can. This means that there's no point in trying to cheat or trying to get a new hand. Just like most people are struggling with some issues about looks, relationships, money, or career, a lot of HSP´s have a problem accepting their sensitivity. Probably because we are a minority and because we are living in a world of non-HSPs!

I know there are children who are blessed with highly conscious parents who give them space and understanding to be a Highly Sensitive, and that is just beautiful. The rest of us, however, have to reframe our whole lives because we were taught that we were abnormal or wrong. The paradox is that we are talking about something that is our most natural state of being and has been all along. It is just that no one ever taught us how to befriend our traits, align ourselves with them, learn how to cooperate with them, use them, and enjoy all their benefits!

It took me some time to realize that there was nothing wrong with the cards I was dealt, but I needed to play quite a few rounds to get to that point. I guess you could say that I was frequently hanging around gamblers who shuffled and gave me new cards that I tried to play. And, trust me, I really tried to win. Not to mention my hopeless tries to cheat! For those of you who are highly sensitive or who know an HSP, you also know that cheating is not an option, so of course this didn't do me any good. And after I had been playing these ruthless games for quite a few years, I thank God that it wore me out!

So, let's simply put the deck of cards to the side and take a look instead at the cards you already have. Take a good look at them because they are the gateway to the freedom of being a Highly Sensitive! We are about to bring forth all the beauty in the traits that most HSP's are lucky to have. We just need to put our focus on the right things. Let's kill the illusion that you only win with a royal straight flush. Play well, and you will win with a pair of fives!

Now if you have some weird and funny ideas about being a Highly Sensitive, you have to be willing to release them and let them go. You see, in order to change, HSPs have to start to see themselves as normal. But when a vessel is already filled to the brim, it's not easy to add anything new, right? So you just need to be willing to let go of all your old ideas about yourself as you read this book, and make up your mind that you are normal already! This new belief will form the foundation of a new sense of confidence and self-esteem and is the most important thing you can do for yourself. So if you encounter people who make it a habit to judge you, make it a habit to leave!

I also have to say that the more you speak up about your own sensitivity and the way you experience life, the more you will start to act like a magnet. You will be amazed by all the people who

Be ok with some people never fully understanding me. Weird = of Faith + spirit.

are out there who not only understand you, but also respect you, for the perfect sensitive way you are, without trying to make you fragile, weak or a "weirdo."

In the end of each chapter I will be asking you some questions. This will stir your mind and make you think about how you live and how you can improve your beautiful life as a Highly Sensitive. And how you can make it more fun! So make sure to take your time to really think and then answer the questions. It´s for your own good!

So are you ready to sit down, relax, and take a good look at your cards in the game of life? We are now going to change any kind of aversion you feel towards your hand and transform it into a fun trip of happiness.

Aversion to touch through being v. highly sensitive to it.

And remember, no cheating!

Introduction

One common question I'm often asked is, "How do you know if you are a Highly Sensitive?" So let´s start out and take a good look at some common traits shared by HSPs, so we can erase any kind of doubts before we move on. Remember that you don´t need to have all these traits in order to be considered an HSP, but most people seem to sense who they truly are when they read through the list. Some traits might be stronger than others but even a subtle feeling within should be taken for real. And keep in mind this is not a diagnosis, but rather a description of a set of characteristics that you can embrace and love.

Some common traits for Highly Sensitive People:

1. You easily get disturbed by light, noises, smells or too many sensory inputs – in fact they can make you really tired. *[Sensory overload]*
2. You tend to avoid crowds of people and if unavoidable you most probably get exhausted. *[over stimulated]*
3. You seem to do things worse when observed. *[Judgement]*
4. You tend to pick up other people´s emotions and seem to know how people are doing and what they need. *[Empathic]*

Margin annotations (left side, handwritten):
- Honest to the core
- Overload of information
- Subtle nuances.
- Perfectionist
- over-stimulated
- over-exposed to negativity
- Balance + pacing self to recharge batteries
- No NLP abuse, brutality
- Structure + routine
- visual + auditory senses aroused
- Trauma
- Sound
- Hold many things personal inside
- Black sheep – a sense "of not fitting in"

5. You are conscientious and loyal to friends, family and employees.
6. You get overwhelmed when too much is going on, especially in stressful situations.
7. You easily register details and subtle information that most people seem to miss out on.
8. You try your hardest to avoid making mistakes.
9. You are easily affected by caffeine, alcohol or by eating too much sugar.
10. You do what you can to stay away from things that upset or overwhelm you.
11. If you have been very busy you often need "downtime" or "alone time" to relax your senses.
12. You tend to feel better when not watching news or violent movies. If you do, they frequently seem to come back in thoughts, memories and dreams.
13. Changes can be difficult for you to go through.
14. You are deeply moved by beautiful art or music.
15. Strong noises can startle you or even cause pain within your body.
16. Your inner life is complex, rich and important to you.
17. You might have an idea that there is something wrong with you.

Now to many, these things might not have the most positive connotation. But keep in mind they are just one part of being a Highly Sensitive and it is simply a lack of understanding of the other aspects of being an HSP.

Whatever you find negative in this world also has a counterpart that is just as powerful. This is when polarity starts to become interesting and fun, right? Sometimes we just have to take a look around to be able to find it.

Now let's dive into the real beauty of being this sensitive person you were born to be.

1. There is nothing wrong with you!

Did you know that when God decided to create human beings he was standing next to an assembly line? The new born babies came along one by one, and he poked every little baby in the belly and said, "You are special!" Then he turned to the next baby, poked it in its belly and said, "You are special!" and so it went on, one baby after another. If you stop and think about it, this is something we all know to be true deep down inside. The evidence is obvious for everyone to see. Some people call them bellybuttons, but I see them as our own unique perfection. Imagine after so many years we are all still simply unique and special in so many ways. And God is obviously keeping up the good work.

Now we are all unique, but we live in a society where the majority of people believe that there are specific things in life that make someone valuable. Unfortunately most people try to adjust to that pre-conceived notion of value:

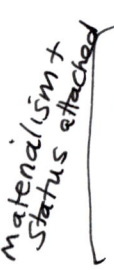

materialism + status attached

being successful, getting married, right after college at 25 (and this is, of course, to your soul-mate,) and having kids, preferably 2.5 to be exact, having a long career, going out and dancing and meeting lots of people, living in a massive house in the middle of the city, throwing pool parties at home twice a week, going to concerts twice a month, maintaining a summerhouse, and a winter house, always travelling and of course having a well behaved dog or two – God forbid if you are allergic. And wait - did I forget to add: looking like you are 25 even though you've already passed 50 and always being happy and energetic?

[margin note: Youthfulness about your purity + innocence]

Okay, now stop and keep in mind that it doesn´t mean that there is something wrong with you if you don´t have any of what I have described above.

You see, if this makes you feel distressed and under even more pressure than anything else, it might be that you are just being influenced by your surroundings. This can at times be stressful, I know, especially if you haven´t got even *one* of the fifteen things I just mentioned.

Many HSPs simply don't fit these criteria most of the time. But, no worries, I have good news for you. There are just as many "truths" about how we should live our lives as there are people.

Scientists say that around 20 % of the population is highly sensitive, so there is no excuse to think that you are alone anymore. As a matter of fact, 20 % of the entire animal kingdom is highly sensitive, so there is no excuse to think that you are abnormal – you have 20 % of all animals on your side as well.

Besides, if people cannot accept the fact that you need a break after you have been doing grocery shopping at rush hour on a Friday afternoon, they simply have a different perception than you.

My point with all this is for you to listen to your inner voice before you try to get into the shoes of the non-highly sensitive and get all stressed out and overwhelmed. I want you to understand that as an HSP it´s okay to feel tired after you have been around a lot of people in an environment filled with sounds, lights, smells, and noises.

When you start to tell people when you have had enough and need a break, you have done your share. By doing this you have taken good care of your-self and this is how you build up stronger personal boundaries that will support and aid you. When you learn how to express your needs, you become a lot more complete and whole as a person and a lot more fun to be around. And a really good side effect to all of this is that you have now given others a chance to help and support you because they have learned what you need.

Margin notes:
- Different perceptions of how to deal with things
- Communicate your needs to others
- Roger + I at freedom meeting – noisy band practise & I had to leave.
- Communicating your needs is a sign of setting v. healthy boundaries & you are allowing others to support you.

You have to tell people what you need, in order for them to be in a position to deliver these to you, if they can.

Just don't expect people to understand your needs without you telling them.

And one more thing, please stop doing any kind of shopping when everybody else does theirs! } *Do your shopping when it is quiet in a shop – beginning/or end of the day!*

Exercise:

Sit down and make sure to write down your dreams as an HSP! } *Dream Journaling*
Listen to your heart and write down the five most important things that you want in your life. } *Writing exercise*
How do you want to live? What kind of work do you wish to do? Are you married? Do you live in an Ashram? Are you a psychic or are you an inventor? Let your heart tell you – and make sure to listen. } *Be open + honest with yourself.*

Make sure to buy a frame. Put your five most important things in it. Hang it up in your bedroom and read it through every morning. Do the same thing every night before you go to bed and let your subconscious dwell on it all night long. } *Visualisation exercise.*

2. See yourself as the Joker, be the wild card

[margin note: Acknowledge that you see things from a v. different perspective than most people.]

As an HSP, you must realize if you haven´t already, that you see things from a totally different angle then most people do. I know that the term HSP is sometimes confused with being introverted, which is not the same thing at all. Scientist say that about 30 % of us HSPs are extroverts, so that kills the HSP = Introvert myth.

[margin note: Intense awareness + data collecting + information like a River. Processing info.]

Most HSPs process information at a very deep level, usually spotting things that probably never crossed the mind of others. It has been proven by scientists that our brains work in a different way, and that we process information on a deeper level.

[margin note: use your voice + knowledge + awareness + share it.]

This is your contribution to the world! Take your experience for real and don´t let anyone take it away from you! Tell people about your knowledge and understanding about a certain thing or topic because most of the time it will enlighten others and show them totally different solutions to any kind of problem.

I have a deeply rooted belief that we were born into this world for a reason, and only you can figure out the reason you were put on this planet. But being quiet and not letting people know who you are and what you think, will not help you find either reason or destiny.

You are doing God + people a dis-service by not sharing your gifts + talents.

Many times I have been hiding in the background observing others because I thought they were doing such a good job already, and also because I found it uncomfortable to speak up and be met with confused looks. You might know the feeling when people sometimes look at you as if they had just spotted a UFO in the skies. If this happens, don´t let it discourage your input. Invite them for a ride in your space ship instead. As I started doing that, I realized that most of the time these people were actually trying to process the information I just gave them. Apparently, it seemed very alien to many of them but instead of judging me, they were sitting with thoughts like, "How the heck did you get that idea?" And most importantly, they didn´t think I was a lunatic.

Awkwardness with speaking up, so I used to slip handwritten notes to people instead.

Invite others into your world.

Silence by others is a processing strategy.

Unique ideas educating in a totally different way.

Highly sensitive´s process information on a deeper level, and to some it might seem weird. This is okay! And all you have to do is to let yourself have your own experience! This processing is valuable information and you can turn it into a real contribution if you share it.

from Cyborg to a tall sunflower! Shine brightly + be seen!!!

"Glow with what you know!"

19

Exercise:

Do you hold yourself back when it comes to ideas or do you spontaneously share them with others?

If you tend to keep your ideas to yourself, what can you do in order to turn this around?

3. Enjoy your sensitivity and others will as well

It´s well known that when you accept and enjoy yourself, people around you will accept you as well. If you were born into this world with high sensitivity I am sure it was to enjoy it! God, your parents, Source, Spirit, or whatever you might want to call it seemed to have created and delivered us without a manual, but I think God decided life would be much too mundane if everything was predictable and choices were obvious. That would take away all the fun! To discover and create our own personal "how-to" manual is to learn, grow, and expand as human beings.

If you refuse to accept who you truly are, it might be difficult to really enjoy your sensitivity, but once you do, you open up doors in all directions.

For example, it drove me nuts for many years that I couldn´t drink an extra cup of coffee or eat that second slice of cake without feeling nauseous or ill the next day. And I tried for many years to drink alcohol only to end up sick, often for days. Now, to drink and eat something that made me sick was obviously not a very loving act to my dear body, my temple. So I started to reevaluate my behaviors and I thought: "Who wants to drink alcohol anyway? Why get numbed by some poison that makes most of us show all the parts of ourselves that we don´t have the guts to show otherwise?"

So I decided to study the effects of alcohol, (both personally and through observation, with various results) and I came to the conclusion that we can be honest, happy, and whole without it. Another result from this rather sloppily performed study is that a lot of people got very agitated that I chose not to drink at all. Once again, I became the outsider - but at least I had the courage to question the behavior a lot of people find so important in life and experience what it was like to leave it behind and to live life "wide awake."

My suggestion to you and what I think most HSPs can do if the desire for caffeine is still there: drink a tiny cup of coffee (just make sure it is not an espresso – or God forbid, a double.). Also keep in mind that nowadays it´s possible to get a decaf.

Instead of eating a small size of that sugar bomb or cake at the party you can always bring some fruit for dessert. But if you have to, just take a small bite of that rich dessert - a lovely side effect is that you will not gain any weight!

At the bar you can simply order a fruit drink and tell them to leave out the alcohol. I have made it a fun habit to challenge the bartenders to create new alcohol free drinks if I go out. Just tell them to make you a liquid fruit salad without alcohol! If someone buys you a drink, you can just stick your tongue into the glass or use a straw and pretend to drink so you can avoid getting sick or suffering from a bad hangover the next day.

If you go to a concert make sure to really enjoy it by letting your deep emotions flow through you as you listen to the music. Get so into it that you have to pinch yourself in the arm and ask yourself whether you or the person on stage is the real singer!

Use your ability to connect on a deeper level of understanding with people and slowly show them who you truly are.

Let your senses fill you completely, and let the beauty seduce you in your everyday life. Let your senses deliver all the sublimity, and rely on your internal alarm. And make sure to trust your body when it´s time to leave.

Exercise:

Sometimes we get caught up in what others do or expect of us. Do you know what amuses you or are you trying to live up to someone else´s ideals?

If you don´t want to go out too much, what would you like to do instead? Make a list of 20 things that make you smile or give you pleasure and make it your intention to include at least three of those things into your life every day – even if it's for a short period of time.

4. Acceptance, your best friend.

Throughout the years I was very concerned with trying to figure out why my body hurt, and why at times my body was really killing me. Some days I couldn´t even walk to the store without getting a bad pain somewhere in my body! This led me to need to rest quite often like some retired 90 year-old.

Many times I had to stop and relax wherever I found something to sit on. But I usually found really nice company and ended up in places and met people I had never expected. So, in my experience, your body will tell you when something is not right. The tricky part is to figure out what it is.

This happened a lot when I met people in a state of fear or who were in a bad mood, so I decided to give myself the right to leave whenever this started to happen. What I didn´t know at the time was that I was then actually trying to escape my own greatness.

I used to walk into a flea market nearby and always ended up with the most horrible back ache and immediately had to leave. It was filled with stagnated energy, and it would probably have taken me weeks to bring things to light. This was before I had gained the understanding that I was trying to protect myself from the feelings of others. I simply didn´t want to accept that I was capable of feeling the feelings of others.

If you are not aware of how much your surroundings affect your wellbeing, you might, like me, try to ignore or escape what's going on around you. But what we resist will also persist! My pain didn't leave me until I was ready to accept that I was carrying not only my own feelings, emotions, and aches but also those which belonged to others. But what a happy discovery! What a happy day! It was finally possible for me to learn how to relax and let it all go, and as I did, my body aches vanished as if some spell had been broken.

I know this sounds "woo-hoo" to many, but this is actually an advantage for Highly Sensitive´s. You pick up on the energy being transmitted from others very easily, and the faster you learn how to accept that this goes on between people at all times, the easier it will get. You are registering something that most people miss!

It is important to take it step by step and to find out what belongs to you and what belongs to others. If things get too intense, I recommend you focus on the feelings that deliver happiness and make you thrive until your boundaries get clearer to you. Approach it as a step by step process, and try asking yourself whether what you're experiencing belongs to you or to somebody else. Resist the temptation to be critical of your physical or emotional experiences and just observe your process. Some things might overwhelm you like dating or meeting new people. But we all need support, and for God´s sake don´t stop dating, just make up your mind to be very selective, and make it your intention to date and meet mature and understanding people.

A pet is also a very good companion, and could be a solution until that right person comes along. So no need to stress! Pets give you unconditional love, and can really adjust to your pace, unless they need to go out for a pee around four in the morning. In that case I would recommend a cat because they usually stay out all night, or sleep it through.

According to experts, pets are prone to reduce stress levels and boost our immune systems against colds and flues. They are also great companions and beautiful for kids to grow up with.

Exercise:

We all get influenced by our surroundings, highly sensitive or not the difference is how we react to certain things. The next time you notice an unpleasant physical or emotional reaction when you are with others, resist the temptation to judge yourself and ask yourself the following questions:

What is causing me to react this way?

What kind of environment am I in?

What kind of an impact is it having on me?

Who is around me and what is happening?

Does this physical or emotional sensation belong to me or does it belong to others?

Is my experience originating from within or from my surroundings?

What can I do to be more comfortable? How can I reduce my stress levels so that I can feel better and think more clearly?

5. Laser focus

Concentration is a skill you've got to learn now if you didn't have the opportunity and support to practice focusing your thoughts as a child. But remember, everything you believe you can also achieve. When you start to direct and use your focus and concentration, on what really matters to you, it will ignite and fuel a fire from within, just like a beam of sunlight that is focused through a magnifying glass, eventually can start a fire in dry grass. This fire within is called your passion.

Some awesome side benefits to this are that you will be able to use your natural intelligence more effectively and be more present with what you do. You are strengthening the muscle that helps you make good choices in life, and you will find it easier to shut things out that might disturb or distract you.

I know, as an HSP it's sometimes very good to listen to three conversations at the same time…..or at least two. It's a gift at parties, and you don't miss a thing. But don't do it at the expense of your own energy level.

Developing your ability to focus well will not only help you direct your energy where you want to, but it will also aid you whenever you are being challenged by some old negative behavior. If you make it a habit to hold on to your object of focus, you will be greatly rewarded. As an HSP, I would guess that your mood can be greatly impacted by others. But as you develop your ability to concentrate and focus you will quickly experience the benefits of being able to stay on track with what's most important to you. You'll be able to prove to yourself that you have the determination to overcome any conscious or subconscious distractions so you can stay on the path towards what you really want in life.

Once you have your focus in order, you will have a much more relaxing time with your friends, your partner, and your family. And it will be easier to separate the different roles you play in life so that you don't get overwhelmed by thoughts that threaten to take you in too many different directions at the same time, leading to stress and confusion. Let work be work, and leave it as you go home. Let family be family and your partner be your partner. Once you put your whole focus on your partner, any relationship will skyrocket and take both of you to the moon.

Exercise:

Stop at several times each day and ask yourself where your focus lies most of the time.

Are you able to be present with someone 100 % or do you tend to always keep a back door open, to listen to what might happen around the two of you?

If so, how can you make yourself snap back into the conversation?

6. Jump into your emotional boat & and rock it!

A lot of HSPs like to spend time alone, partly because we need downtime, but also because it´s a good time to be creative and philosophical. I do too, but I recommend you let the people surrounding you see you come up to the surface once in a while! Be like the little man that jumps out of the box when someone pushes the button every now and then.

Let your emotional richness be expressed to its full extent. Your emotions are the most natural part of you – the language of your subconscious. And they are supposed to flow in order for us to feel well.

When you exercise the courage to show your emotions, you serve as a positive example for others who may be afraid to show how *they* feel. You can serve as a role model and a reminder that life is more than just a series of dull everyday moments, and also that a good cry is both a release and an expression of your truth. Who doesn´t want to cry with happiness?

Some might think you are manic depressive at times, but so what? Just because they are afraid of emotions doesn´t mean that you have to hide yours. You are swinging the pendulum, and, if you have had a rough time, just relax and follow the swing as it pushes you right back up to the top again.

Even though it might feel scary at first, expressing your emotions will help you win in the game of life – it is like betting all you own in a poker game when you have a royal straight flush in your hand – you simply cannot lose!

Not only are you showing people that you can have strong emotions and still be alive and kicking, but you are also paving the way for those who are afraid to allow their own feelings come up to the surface!

Exercise:

How easy is it for you to express your emotions?

If it's difficult, how can you start to express your emotions without judging yourself?

What are the benefits of a good cry?

What are other ways to release your emotions in a healthy way?

How can expressing your own emotions help others to release theirs?

7. Trust your vibes

As an HSP there might be certain things you feel you simply cannot do. This can become either a blessing or a curse depending on how you handle it.

Just imagine: how are you ever going to become over weight if you cannot eat sugar or fast food? Your body keeps protesting when you feed it something useless. Since your body doesn't speak in words it has to communicate to you in some other form. Trust these vibes. The chance is that you will probably become a health guru without even having to think about it.

When I didn't eat meat, people who invited me for dinner always got overly concerned that I wouldn't be pleased or have enough to eat to feel satisfied. This made a lot of people nervous.......and I mean really nervous, so whoever said that it only happens to HSPs is obviously wrong!

Now, your body is smart, and it will easily tell you what hurts and what doesn't. It is your great teacher and companion through life. It took me a while to really start listening to these signals. At times, I forgot or ignored the fact that two pieces of sweet cake would give me a hang over the next day (but this was before I could really appreciate my own sensitivity.)

Your body is your temple, and it's the physical expression of your own mind. A sensitive mind equals a sensitive body! Use your senses and take them seriously! They are talking to you in a language that you will have to learn sooner or later! You owe it to yourself and your body to put your needs first.

If you decide to learn the language of your vibes, many new careers can open up for you. You can work as a psychic, healer, health guru, or massage therapist as it simply comes very naturally to you! Your vibes are your strength - make sure to listen to them.

Exercise:

What kind of a relationship do you have with your own body?

Is it your best friend or someone you try to fight at times?

What is it that you do in particular, that makes your whole body relax and feel safe together with you?

8. Party tricks

Most HSPs don´t want to go to over-crowded, loud parties where people drink or smoke a lot, but if you ever get talked into it you should try to hit Halloween for a good trick. You can always show up early and leave when it´s time.

Use your sensitivity as you usually do. This means to pick up emotions, aches, and other rarities from other people.

Dress up like Superman, Spiderman, or Jason from Friday the 13th. You could wear the mask from the movie "Scream" or if you prefer, be the Hulk. If you do the latter three you could sneak up to people and tell them about their feelings and aches and pains, and simply shock them for a good trick.

If you want to do the nicer version of this, you might want to dress up like Gandhi, Mother Teresa, Jesus, or Buddha and spread your love by acknowledging other people's aches and then at the same time heal them.

Some people might not take you seriously, since it is a costume party, but I bet they will be surprised when they have sobered up the next morning and happen to remember you talking about their aches and pains and the deep seated emotions that they never told anyone about.

Exercise:

If you were to throw a party, what would it look like?

What could you do in order to have a nice time with your friends at home?

How would you use your unique abilities to make "the" party?

9. Not good for you? Then dump it!

Stress is a big challenge in society today. We see and meet people everywhere who are under some sort of stress, and we all pay a high price doing it. Some want to call it positive stress, and if that is their choice of putting it I will leave it at that.

I have the belief that stress is not good for anyone unless it's because you are standing eye to eye with a lion or a mugger in a dark alley. When we don't have the ability to feel relaxed on a daily basis, it's more of a constant tiring state of fear than a state of being in control of the situation. Constant fear and anxiety can freeze your whole body and put your system on hold.

When you start to feel stressed or get too influenced by the people around you who are filled with stress, please give yourself permission to leave. Why stay in an environment that is not good for you? Your body is giving you signals that there is a lot going on, and you can choose to avoid the negative Impact of other people's stress by either accepting it as energy that is not your own and letting it pass through you or by leaving the premises!

Some might think this is very selfish, but ask any adult why they don't eat the green peas, liver or cow tongue at a smorgasbord, and they will answer, "I simply don't like it." It is a consciously made choice, and you are allowed to give yourself permission to do what feels right and what tastes good from the smorgasbord of life.

I was waiting for the bus to the airport one day, and, as soon as the bus stopped and the door opened, I was hit by an enormous wall of stress. I sat down up front and it was amazing to see everyone on board very much on edge. It was as if someone had emptied an enormous bag of ants in there and they seemed to be crawling all over people making them itch and scratch. It convinced me that we are all more or less very sensitive, and that we are all very easily influenced by what surrounds us, since I was not able to spot a calm soul in the whole bus.

I heard that the bus was late and we were expecting delays. The poor bus driver was more or less hysterical. I had no choice but to sit in the bus totally soaked in massive stress, and at that moment, I was very grateful that I had been practicing meditation and focus for many years.

I decided to meditate my way both to the airport, all the way to my flight and was focusing on using my breath to completely blow away all the anxiety surrounding me. Indeed, we were delayed, but I managed both to check-in my bag 15 minutes before departure and to catch my flight.

In situations like this, it is great to be able to know what stress is, and, to discern when it belongs to someone else, for then you are able to leave it behind. Stress is not good for you, so use your sensitivity to minimize it and try as soon as possible to find out if it´s yours or if it´s coming from someone else. If you have doubts and are not sure if you are being influenced or if you originated the stress, close your eyes and ask yourself if this stems from you. Then carefully listen, and let your intuition give you the answer. Your intuition is a better guide than your mind, since it always shows up first -before your mind starts reasoning.

Try to see your body and mind as a bag that is completely full with your own stuff, so it´s impossible to fit in any more. Unless you are in good company, always try to keep the bag full and protect yourself from taking on more than you want to handle. Let others carry their own stuff!

Exercise:

Ok unless you are standing in front of a lion or almost got run over by a truck – stress is simply not good for your system.

What does stress do to you? How does it make you feel? Make a clear description of it and share it, as I think it would give others bright new inputs.

Do you often leave your bag halfway empty or can you consciously fill it up with yourself?

If halfway empty – what personal qualities would you choose to fill your bag?

How can these qualities help you reduce the stress in your life and live more peacefully no matter what the surrounding circumstances?

10. Be the mentor!

Some HSPs have a tendency to be very uncomfortable around a lot of people. This trait can be misinterpreted by a lot of people who tend to see us as meditators, gurus, or some bearded hermit living in a cave whether we practice solitude and meditation in our lives or not. A lot of us spend time alone in calm environments, reflecting on our own thoughts and ideas.

There is always a way out of situations and things that are stressful and causing us problems in life. Imagine that you are blessed with a natural ability to see insights and answers for others who are not as tuned to the possibilities that are all around us. Imagine that it is natural for you to notice and experience miracles!

So a good way to use this could be to teach meditation! If you decide to teach meditation, you can always choose to have a limited number of students, not become overwhelmed, and still make a positive impact on other people.

A lot of HSPs have a naturally calm demeanor and a hawk´s eye for what is needed in their surroundings. This can be used to help people relax and calm down so you can guide them to find their own peace within. What a beautiful way to help others reduce their stress by using your natural gifts and talents!

If you decide to teach meditation, another important point is that yoga and meditation studios are usually not located in busy stressful places, as they are meant to provide a sacred space for the customers. Another option is to find the perfect spot and start your own studio to provide peace of mind for others and be a good leader and teacher with your natural presence.

Exercise:

We all need downtime and that is a normal coping strategy for our body to regain balance.

What is it during downtime that helps you recover?

What do you do then?

Share your insights with others as you can be of big help!

11. Let your-self flip out and be creative

For some reason, my mind has always been a few steps ahead of me and I have often found myself dealing with too many ideas at once. Sometimes I feel I have to address all the ideas, but then I need to balance myself with rest so I will not become too overwhelmed. Being an extrovert and an HSP is not always an easy combination.

With a mind that moves as quickly as a rabbit, (where I usually manage to see more than five perspectives in a matter of seconds,) I discovered that I have a variety of ways to express my creativity. At times I have found myself telling stories that made even my most talkative friends become quiet. I also keep a booklet in my purse at all times to be able to write any ideas that spontaneously pops up in my mind.

It can also be a beautiful outlet from time to time to splash or smudge a canvas with oils. If right handed, paint with your left hand, with your fingers or maybe even with your eyes closed. Take a singing class. Write a novel, a song or a book. Learn how to play an instrument. Build a webpage. Refurnish your apartment or paint your house. Jump up and down on a trampoline, or at least have the guts to stick more than your toes into the cold ocean water at summer time.

It might be very uncomfortable at first, but it will also kick you forward in life! You will begin to realize all the stuff you are capable of doing even when others have assumed that you couldn´t. Usually, these adrenalin kicks affect me a lot and I experience that I expand as a person when I jump out of my comfort zones every now and then.

Exercise:

Letting your creativity flow will help you maintain a balance. Tap into your inner creator and let your magnificent ideas flow.

In what way are you using your creativity?

Write down the five most important projects you have been dreaming about accomplishing – then start with number one.

12. Sex

Sex for an HSP is, when respected and shared with deep understanding, worth more than a fortune. As a matter of fact, it *is* a fortune, a treasure and a goldmine! I think most HSPs agree with me because, once we do something, we tend to do it well.

Your partner has to be well informed about your sensitivity, and you have to express your boundaries clearly because becoming overwhelmed in bed can quickly turn into a nightmare. You need to explain what, in particular, feels good and what you enjoy the most. But you also need to let your partner know when or how you want to do it! Help your partner understand the depth of your needs, and once you open Pandora´s box, no one will ever want to leave you.

Not only do HSPs process information on a deeper level, but they also, when happy, are a lot happier than non-HSPs. So make up your mind to use this awesome sensitivity, and let yourself explore your sex life in a totally new way. I don´t know about you, but to me as an HSP an orgasm is not simply an orgasm, and the more you have the guts to explore your own sensitivity, the higher and deeper you will ride the wave.

You might want to make it a habit to find new sensitive spots to be touched or maybe a new exciting place to complete the act itself. In this case, I do have to underline the importance that your partner knows all about your sensitivity! This communication will eliminate any misunderstanding, if your partner wants to take you to a rose garden or do it in public. (Unless, of course, you are into some extra pain or enjoy being watched!).

So for good, hot sex, good communication is step one. After that, you can just tie yourself to the rocket and fire it off.

Let your sensitivity guide you, and afterwards, as you rest, try to explain to your partner about the tingling feeling HSPs have in every little cell after a good performance together with your loved one. But I am also warning you because this will make them want to do it over and over again!

Exercise:

Don´t expect your partner to be a mind reader. Be open about your needs to create clarity!

Are you communicating your needs clearly to your partner? If not, how could you improve?

Do you remember to keep a balance between giving and receiving?

13. Use your accuracy

As long as no one is looking over our shoulder and, if we are not being disturbed by a lot of inputs, deep concentration can become the most natural thing to a Highly Sensitive Person. However, to try to do things while being observed can disturb many of us and cause us to feel out of balance.

When we have a chance to do our work undisturbed, most of us tend to easily focus on the details, and we are often quick and precise.

Some of us are like well-trained dogs searching for mines or pigs looking for truffles, and we seem to have the capacity to detect problems and challenges long before they appear. As a matter of fact, they often pop up together with the idea itself. This can of course create difficulties for others to follow you, but keep in mind to just stay on course and recognize your own way of finding valuable information and make a decision to trust it!

You might not have been taught to see this trait as such a good thing, but when you learn how to share it, you will see that to others it can truly be a goldmine. This is just another reminder and encouragement that your point of view can, many times, enrich other people´s lives if you decide to share it and not just keep it to yourself.

See it as your own ability to open up new realms for others, while pointing out the details you just discovered.

Some of us HSPs have a tendency to have thoughts and feelings running 2000 miles an hour within our brains. Sharing this is a good way to relieve a lot of this speed from our inner system. I have personally come to see it as a perfect outlet that reduces any sort of overload.

Commit to yourself to share all your ideas for the next week, no matter how awkward they seem to others and feel how this affects you.

Exercise:

Are you letting people hear your point of view when a matter is discussed?

Do you know what your own outlets are, so you can release stress and speed from your inner system?

Try to share more of your insight for the next week or so and see what happens.

14. Love it – it´s for free!

Many HSPs have a very strong intuition. As a matter of fact, our sensitivity IS our intuition, so to take it seriously is highly essential. For some of us, it´s so strong that we most likely have been living by it all our lives without even knowing! An HSP asking about her intuition is like a fish asking about water. It simply comes so naturally to her that it´s a part of her being.

Once I was waiting for a flight in Frankfurt. I was sitting down reading a good book. There were a lot of announcements, as always, at the airport, but the book was good, and I managed to keep my focus. All of a sudden, my body got up and I had no clue what was going on. I was kind of shocked as I found myself standing up for no good reason with the book in my hand. But, as I sat down again, I took a break from the book and started to listen to the announcements. My flight was overbooked and people were being offered $650 just to take the next flight a few hours later. Not a bad deal. Now, I was totally wrapped up in my good book, but my intuition got the message and quickly told my body to pay attention and act!

Most of you have probably had the experience of thinking about someone at some point in your life, and then five minutes later you run into them around the corner. Or maybe you pick up your phone to call someone, and at the same time they call you.

This is not a bad way to save yourself some phone bills!

Try tuning into your intuition before you meet someone. You'll probably find that you can sense their emotions way ahead of the meeting and will not be surprised about whatever they are going to tell you.

Exercise:

We are all intuitive beings but being highly sensitive is a huge plus as intuition is just another word for it.

Do you recognize your intuition?

Do you trust your inner wisdom?

How has your intuition helped you throughout life?

15. Who could possibly be bored?

For many years, I was very impatient. I literally had ants in my pants and wanted things to move quickly and preferably move my way! A lot of my friends have a totally opposite style, and it used to be if I didn´t get a quick enough answer, at least within two seconds, I thought they hadn't 't heard me or weren´t listening.

Little did I know how I could, and would, finally transform my enormous impatience into a somewhat more calm and relaxed personality. As a matter of fact, today I am the one who usually stays calm in most situations.

As I was running and hiding from my sensitivity, I was living a pretty stressful life, and I did find a lot of situations boring and without any stimulating action. Then I started meditating and taking good care of myself, and, as my internal pace started to slow down, I could suddenly see my surroundings. I realized that flowers are beautiful - that they smell good, and I could even hear birds singing. It opened a whole new world to me of sounds, tastes, noises, feelings, and smells. Of course, all of these sensory inputs can present themselves in a wide range of intensity which can be overwhelming at times, but it most certainly never gives me a feeling of being bored any longer. There is always something to look at, listen to, smell, or feel no matter where I go.

One day, when I was still working as a prison guard, I had to follow an inmate to the hospital. We had to wait for the doctor and ended up staying in the lobby for about six hours. It took my inmate friend about five minutes to look through the 200 magazines surrounding us, and then his legs started jumping. For me, the whole day was just a long meditation. I was calm and relaxed, and every now and then I looked up at the people coming through.

This world is filled with information in every moment, and your sensitivity will help you be attuned to the interesting experiences happening all around you if you relax and open yourself up to receiving.

Exercise:

Highly Sensitive's are skilled in finding details.

Do you give yourself time to find the beautiful details around you?

How can you remind yourself to stop throughout the day stop and smell the flowers or simply breathe in the fresh air?

16. Build rapport – because you can.

We all want to feel loved for who we really are. Don´t we all have a desire to feel special in some way? Most people want to be liked by the people they come in contact with, right? And, to be realistic, most of us don´t like to have conflicts simply for the heck of it (yes, I know there are a few exceptions.)

Your sensitivity is your strength in many ways. You have the ability to see things that most people don´t. This also gives you the opportunity to observe and share the beauty you see in people. With your hawk eye, you probably notice any little change in your friend´s home, in their garden, or even in the behavior of their dog. You probably see every little change in a person. This could mean anything from new clothes, to a new style, a haircut, weight loss, etc. You might observe that little scar on their chin that most people miss, and if you let that person know how charming you find it they will not only feel special but also feel your presence.

Now, let me give you a few warnings, though. It is a good idea to leave out comments about differences that are too obvious (like a lost front tooth or a black eye!). Go for the subtle details, for this is where your strength lies.

Also, be careful about commenting on any sort of injury you might notice. Someone might feel uncomfortable and embarrassed if you comment that they all of a sudden started to walk kind of funny. Trust me, I am telling you this out of my own experience!

Focus on the little things that make every person unique in their own way. It's a quick and simple way to build rapport and help people to feel special. They'll love you for it!

Exercise:

The trick to build rapport is to find the beauty in details and simply love them.

Do you ever tell others what you really like about them?

Do you let yourself receive all the good you hear from others?

17. Tell your imaginative stories

Whatever you do, dear sensitive, never put the lid on your imagination. You are most likely one of the people who has an incredibly quick and ever working imagination. Once you break through the terror barrier and realize that you can step up and be seen in a way that is comfortable for you (since sensitive´s can be introverted or extroverted) you will be able to use your skill to impress your friends, family and colleagues – and the whole world!

I have been in situations where I have told stories and have at times totally let my imagination flip out and guide me, and, to my surprise, people have loved it. It´s like an adrenalin rush because the imaginative information is always swirling around us. All we need to do is grab a hold of it and start using it. And once you start to use it and share it with others you will notice new doors opening for you.

This last summer, I was privileged to hold a wedding ceremony for friends, and I realized that when I try to do something correctly or perfectly, especially when observed by others, I usually screw it up. When HSPs are observed, and if we haven´t cultivated our focus we seem to lose our abilities. So I decided to simply use my imagination and let it guide me through this whole ceremony, which I did, and it all went beautifully.

If you feel like you are not ready to take the plunge at a party or on a date, I recommend you practice with kids. They are so loving and interested in your attention and usually have the same kind of imaginative skills, so you can probably collaborate with ease. You will most certainly get some inspiration and fun ideas as well.

Exercise:

Through our imagination we can create a great deal and have a lot of fun!

What was the last thing you imagined?

Are you using your imagination in a specific way?

Do you use it on a daily basis?

18. Bring forth your "weirdness"

Thank god there are kids that grow up in a very conscious environment where sensitivity is the most natural thing and nothing is odd. Unfortunately, a lot of us had to grow up listening to the opposite, but this feeling of being odd or not fitting in anywhere is something you can turn into your strength.

A lot of times we need personal experiences to understand another person. It is always easy to tell someone to get their act together, but a lot of times you hear that from a person who is not very accepting of themselves in the first place. Feeling odd and misunderstood is not very pleasant for anyone, but if you had this experience growing up or if you have had this feeling throughout your life you also know what it means to be an outcast.

If you were going through a challenging time and had to struggle, it probably makes you more humble when seeing others struggle. There is a reason the second name for an HSP is "empath," or someone who can really feel what the other person is going through.

Use this skill with other people who might need a helping hand. Once you connect with an outcast, you will realize that they are simply good, loyal friends once you bond. To a certain extent, I think this can be done in any relationship, and as you share your path, this can also turn into a blessing to others.

Exercise:

How are you using your earlier experiences as a Highly Sensitive in your life?

Write down all the times you have been able to help others and see the magnificence and beauty in doing it!

19. Talk away about your Royal HSP title

Things are changing, and I cannot say it too many times that when you speak up about your own truth you also get in contact with your own power. If you don´t already, you have to start to believe that this power is yours at all times. This is a gift that you can learn how to use. But first comes first, you need to fully accept who you are!

Anyone who is doing something for the first time might not be very convincing, but the more you practice, the easier it will become. According to some psychologists, HSPs tend to develop their sensitivity and focus too much on other people, forgetting about themselves. This might be true to a certain extent, but probably more often because we are humble and aware of the other person and haven´t been taught to speak our own truths.

This is highly essential to learn.

In my experience, I was taught to care for others and was not taught how to really take care of myself, and it has been quite a lesson to learn as an adult. Today, as I have gained clarity on myself and my needs, it´s easier to be present as who I am and stay true to what's important to me.

But I have found that my sensitivity is still the same though. I might not pick up the same extreme amount of information from others because I have learned to let some of it go. I also now know my boundaries a lot better and I prefer not to challenge them. But I still notice my surroundings and what people feel and carry with them to a certain extent.

People with little or no understanding are most likely not able to tell us what to do. And we are often told to simply STOP being sensitive. Sorry Mac, it doesn´t work that way, your sensitivity is here to stay. But the better you get to know it and embrace it – the more of its beauty you will experience.

> Melanie "You need to toughen up!"
> – Or perhaps "you need to soften down."

As a matter of fact, it was fascinating to realize that when I started to share about myself and my traits of sensitivity, I built my own power by not trying to be like everybody else. It´s pretty reasonable right?

But, no matter how much I focus, I am still a sensitive person that processes information deeply and I will always pick up on a lot of the subtle information around me from both people and my environment.

As I write this, I just had a tiny cup of coffee at home. After a few sips, my heart started racing. But this is not because I am afraid of drinking a cup of coffee but that my body simply registers the effect of the substance in my body.

So, this sensitivity does not simply disappear just because I step up and speak my truth, but it *has* caused me to learn how to communicate clearly with people who are not as sensitive and might not have any experiences dealing with Highly Sensitive People.

And, to me, frequent coffee drinking or going to concerts three nights in a row would probably cause my nervous system to freak out. It´s simply not worth it! Period!

Exercise:

Have you fully befriended your traits as a Highly Sensitive or are you still waiting for the moment when (you hope) it´s going to disappear?

Do you see why self-knowledge is your best friend in order to accept the traits you have?

20. A trillion ways! Which one is yours?

If someone tried to tell you what to do and how to live or tell you not to be so sensitive it might be because they simply don't understand you and how you function. It´s like going to a course to learn how to ride a horse from someone who has never seen one. You would probably end up facing its tail while getting up on the horseback. It´s like having an over-weight person teach you all about health and diet, or it might feel like trying to find a needle in a haystack.

We all have our answers within, but we have to take a personal responsibility to listen to our inner voice and find them for ourselves.

Once we pin-point our own uniqueness, it´s ours to hold on to and whatever we do, we can't let it go!

Try looking at the world with the perspective that everyone has something unique to offer. If you continue to resist your own sensitivity, or hang around people who don´t understand it, it will probably be difficult to find and hold on to your own unique qualities. Be aware that your gifts and talents might at first make themselves known as a silent whisper, so, if you are not used to listening to your inner voice, don´t expect it to be loud as if from a megaphone. As a matter of fact, if you constantly shut out your inner voice, it will literally start to express itself in some other way - such as a pain in your body.

We might have to make a few more choices in order to understand our own path. But keep in mind that the path is never ending. Let your feelings guide you to take one step in front of the other.

Some of us just have to keep on trying until we find it, but please take my word for it. If you dive into the search for your own inner treasures you will eventually find the gold!!

Exercise:

Before you go to bed tonight, write down the question:

What is my uniqueness?

Say it out loud a few times and keep your focus on it. Then go to bed and let your subconscious help you out and deliver you an answer.

21. Pioneer the world

I had a discussion with a friend who is a psychologist and who is working with people who have pushed their limits to such a high degree that they simply cannot work anymore. As we talked, he seemed to have the impression that a lot of these people didn´t have healthy boundaries and were hypersensitive (mainly because of bad parenting in childhood) and that was the reason why people couldn´t stop before they ended up sick.

But stop and think about what happens when you have pulled a muscle and still keep on running. Most of us would experience bad injuries by doing this. And what if this is your way of becoming aware of who you truly are? What if this is one way of finding your boundaries? It is not necessarily true that people develop an extreme sensitivity because we go to the wrong kind of job for too long. It might throw a lot of us out of balance, which might have given us symptoms like hypersensitivity, but this can happen to anyone who keeps on pushing their limits too hard for too long.

What if this is just the approach some psychologists have because they do not understand this sensitivity themselves? It would be similar to a person who drinks and smokes a lot trying to tell you how exceptionally well they love and treat themselves. Or would you take a cooking class from a teacher who has never cooked food?

I think people often look for some sort of an experience with another person in order to feel understood. If you are not interested or don't like someone, you will most likely do a better job without them. I have a belief that most HSPs can, through their intuition, feel when something is genuine or not, and it's important to listen to that signal from within.

High Sensitivity is not a disease. It is a trait you are born with, just as some children are born with blue eyes and others with green eyes. Some even have one green and one brown, but it still doesn't make it a disease!

My point is: stop fighting against the sensitivity and accept both the positive aspects and the challenging ones. It seems to me that some people (usually non-HSPs) simply expect sensitivity to go away when we find a balance. This fooled me for many years as well, as I was thinking the sensitivity would one day just vanish as if it had never existed.

Instead, I have learned how to put my focus on embracing it and letting it guide me instead of seeing it as a behavior or a thing that I have to change or get fixed.

Exercise:

Do you know your limits or are you still pushing yourself in order to find them? Make a list of all the good things about having boundaries!

22. Your right brain´s genius - spirituality

Let´s take a look at your brain for a second. Your brain consists of two hemispheres, and your body is linked to a cross over system which means that the right side of your body is connected to the left side of your brain and vice versa.

Logic, math and exact calculation, and language functions such as grammar and vocabulary are often lateralized to the left hemisphere of the brain. Some other functions include: detail orientation, form strategies, use of practical solutions and safety.

Left brain functions	**Right brain functions**
Uses logic	Uses feelings
Detail oriented	"Big picture" oriented
Facts rule	Imagination rules
Words and language	Symbols and Images
Present and past	Present and future
Math and science	Philosophy and religion
Can comprehend	Can "get it"

Knows	Believes
Acknowledges	Appreciates
Order/pattern perception	Spatial Perception
Knows an object's name	Knows an object's function
Reality based	Fantasy based
Forms strategies	Presents possibilities
Practical	Impetuous
Safe	Risk taking

Artistic abilities, facial perceptions, and processing of visual and audio stimuli are lateralized to the right hemisphere of the brain. Some other functions include: feelings, symbols and images, present and future orientation and spatial perception.

According to research, HSPs either have a higher activity or a higher blood flow in the right part of the brain or they have an overactive or finely tuned nervous system.

As you probably understand by now, most HSPs are right-brainers and highly spiritual beings! And in a world full of leftbrainers, who often can be very skeptical, it's more important to trust you own traits, signals, and ideas instead of trying to change the whole left-brain world to make them understand you.

You see, when you stand up and live the life you want to, you will attract people to you who are in the same state of mind. Also, your good vibrations will then make others interested in how the heck you do what you do so well, and this is when it's a good time to start explaining how and why you function the way you do.

It's my experience that in order to get understanding, you have to let people come to you and ask you to explain instead of you trying to tell them how to understand you. So the ground rule is to keep focusing on your health, wellness, and your own self. Once you do, the rest will follow!

Exercise:

Go back to the list of right and left brain traits above and take a good look. Check off the traits that describe you best. Whatever you choose you get 1 point. In the end, sum both sides up and see where your highest score lies!

What can you do to leverage your natural inclinations?

What can you do to enhance those traits that you'd like to express but may not come as naturally to you?

23. Dance!

Dear highly sensitive, You Were Born to Master Your Body! And, since HSPs have a finely tuned nervous system, you most likely have finely tuned motor skills as well. You can probably feel every tiny little part of your body, right? Now, who said that sensitivity is not good? This is a gift you have been given. To sense every little part of your body and to feel every little joint, ligament, or muscle also makes you very aware of how you move.

HSPs are often very conscious about their moves and grooves, so, yes, you can apply it not only at the ballet class but in any kind of dance.

Ballet is a suggestion for anyone who wants to dance but might not always want to be close to others. Try a liberating dance like Zumba where everybody just moves around and has fun or try a street dance like break dancing. Do some awesome Michael Jackson grooves and you will probably impress everyone. Tango is also an amazing dance, but some might find it challenging, as body contact is one of the key aspects of dancing a good tango.

Be creative, open up, and express yourself – you might just reach the top. And, when you do, keep in mind that you were .

supposed to be on top and on stage, so get ready for the Cheering audience!

Exercise:

Keep in mind that dancing is moving to vibration. It is a great way to stay fit and to keep a flow in the body and you can dance alone if you want to!

Do you have a favorite dance?

Do you give yourself time to move around daily?

24. The HSP synonym - Intuition

Some people want to separate sensitivity and intuition. You see, we all have an intuition whether we choose to believe it or not. You are still doing things by your intuition on a daily basis whether you realize it or not, so it is not a bad thing to understand that your sensitivity is also your intuition, giving you access to valuable information in your life every day.

Your intuition is showing up in many different shapes and colors. Some hear a little whisper from within while others see pictures within their minds. Don´t be mistaken by thinking that your physical sensitivity is any different from the other types. You can be sensitive in many ways, including: emotional, physical, mental or spiritual. And some people are just still learning to accept the fact that we are spiritual, sensitive beings simply living in a physical body.

Your intuition is your inner guidance, and HSPs are just provided with it more deeply rooted in their finely tuned nervous systems.

Your intuition is providing you with signs and information all the time. Let it be your closest ally. And don´t get it confused with your thoughts – your intuition always shows up like a "hunch" long before your reasoning mind wants a word in the discussion.

Keep in mind that your intuition is guiding you where to go and what to do to expand and grow as a human being, so don´t expect it to only serve things, people, or circumstances that makes you feel good. That would be just as foolish as cheating or trying to change the cards you got in your hand.

Exercise:

Your intuition is quick and clear and shows up first of all.

Do you ever get a feeling of doing something in particular and after a while you seem to talk your way out of it?

Do you ever end up in situations where you knew you should have listened to your first "hunch"?

What can you do to change that?

25. The intelligent influence

Did you know that this world is built upon vibrations, and there is not really a clear separation between either people or things? As a matter of fact, everything is energy, and energy travels beyond time and space. This means that human beings are very easily influenced by their surroundings. Now, being an HSP is a gift in many ways since you are probably more attuned than others to how the world influences you. A lot of times we need a personal experience to believe things like this. Now this makes it obvious, if you don´t have the experience, you are less likely to believe it.

When you let it sink in, you will probably realize what an incredible insight it is to know how we all affect each other. Most people are not aware of this, and therefore, they think they are independent even though they are doing exactly what their surroundings are doing at all times. Some even say that nothing is affecting them because they never have any emotional reactions. This is most definitely a non-HSP talking, and the best thing we can do is just let it go.

Learn to love this insight as it gives you sort of a preview of life. You can quickly detect any kind of danger. You probably know what I mean: when you go to the movies, do you locate the EXIT signs long before you even find your seat? Not because you are afraid of a fire but because you are registering the sign. And did you know that the most sensitive horse in a herd naturally becomes the leader as it easily detects dangers and can quickly bring the rest of the herd to safety?

If you are aware of how easily we are influenced, you most likely also grasp the power you have within to choose to create what you DO want in your life instead of the opposite!

Exercise:

Do you have a tendency to have eyes in your neck and you know how many people just walked into the restaurant behind you without seeing?

Can you recall any situation in your life where you have detected any sort of danger before it actually happened?

26. Smile and laugh every day!

Never underestimate your own humor, and laugh as often as you can. At times, I can recall events and situations that were so hilarious that it´s simply impossible NOT to laugh. So, wherever you are, a good laugh lightens up anything or anyone, and the good thing is - it is contagious. It´s like starting a fire in the forest during dry season and once the match is lit, nothing can extinguish the hungry flames.

Be the hungry flame yourself by looking at the things that make you happy. When you do, you direct your energy exactly where you want to and this makes it grow. As a matter of fact, your happiness grows exponentially as you focus more and more on what you love and what makes you feel good. Your ability to see the humor in even difficult circumstances is a skill that will serve you throughout life and can lead to great success!

There is not really any trick to happiness besides awareness, and that is something HSPs are very good at. So smile, laugh and be glad that you can!

Exercise:

What makes you really happy?

Do you ever share it? If not, I suggest you start right now.

27. Enjoy your recovery

If you have been experiencing challenges in life that have aroused confusing or stressful feelings for various reasons, remember that this can happen to anyone. In times like these it is good to look for ways to reward yourself by practicing self-care.

How about giving yourself a treat every second week? Go to a nice, mild massage therapist, or try aroma therapy. Try Thai Chi, or how about a yoga class for sensitive´s, or maybe even a trip to the sauna? Or you could go to a spa nearby and spend the afternoon in the jaccuzi. Just make sure to go when most people are at work, and pray that the spa is open at a time when you can have some peace and quiet.

Listen to relaxing music, take a walk in nature, praise yourself for being your best friend, and remember that you are allowed to be a loner if you need to be.

As you do, you put yourself first, which is something we should all teach our kids today. You then start to feel very healthy and well and can provide so much more for others.

Be pleased that you can spend a lot of time alone and enjoy it. This is your way of recovering. Keep in mind that a lot of people simply cannot stand their own company so this is a true blessing. Enjoy it!

Exercise:

Your last exercise will be to make sure to take good care of yourself. When was the last time you went to a massage or had a treatment? Do it – you are worth it!

Summary

Now we all want to get on the highway to happiness, right? We all want to be healthy, vibrant and happy. Stop and think for a second, and take these ideas and tips to make everyday worthwhile. You have the power within to make life what you want to, so do not underestimate who you are or what you are capable of doing.

Speak up, talk away, jump into the crowd, get out and let yourself have your daily rest. There is nothing wrong with you and you are definitely not alone. You are perfect and the world needs to know, hear and feel your sensitivity.

Just keep in mind that everything you want to cultivate in life needs your attention and focus. So give yourself the love you deserve for simply being who you are.

Be the unique person you have always been – and you will soon start to accept and love it!

Wherever you put your energy, it will come back to you, multiplied with a flow of resources, so love your sensitivity and be who you were born to be!

Good luck!

Printed in Great Britain
by Amazon.co.uk, Ltd.,
Marston Gate.